ULTIMATE FIDGET SPINNER
Tricks and Tips

Scholastic Canada Ltd.
604 King Street West, Toronto, Ontario M5V 1E1, Canada

Scholastic Inc.
557 Broadway, New York, NY 10012, USA

Scholastic Australia Pty Limited
PO Box 579, Gosford, NSW 2250, Australia

Scholastic New Zealand Limited
Private Bag 94407, Botany, Manukau 2163, New Zealand

Scholastic Children's Books
Euston House, 24 Eversholt Street, London NW1 1DB, UK

www.scholastic.ca

Library and Archives Canada Cataloguing in Publication
Cataloguing in publication data is available for this title.

ISBN: 978-1-4431-3968-7

WARNING: Finger spinners contain small parts and are a choking hazard. They are not for children under 3 years. Keep spinners away from pets and young children. Ensure spinners have been purchased from reputable retailers and were accompanied by age-grading and safety information. Discard any worn or broken spinners immediately.

First published by Carlton Books Limited in 2017.
This edition published by Scholastic Canada Ltd. in 2017.
Text and design copyright © 2017 by Carlton Books Limited.

Written, illustrated, designed and packaged by: Dynamo Limited
Cover illustrations: Shutterstock.com

5 4 3 2 1   Printed in Canada 140   17 18 19 20 21

ULTIMATE FIDGET SPINNER
Tricks and Tips

Scholastic Canada Ltd.
Toronto New York London Auckland Sydney
Mexico City New Delhi Hong Kong Buenos Aires

CONTENTS

THE FIDGET RULES

Make sure your stunts are trouble free with this guide.

1. School rules
Each school has different rules when it comes to fidget spinners. Before you take yours into class, ask your teacher what the rules are at your school. You don't want your favourite spinner to get confiscated before you've even learned your first trick!

2. Space means safe
Make sure you have plenty of room around you. This way, if your spinner flies off in the wrong direction, you can be sure it won't end up lodged in the TV screen! Outside is often a great place to practise stunts.

3. Family fun
Your little brother or sister might think you are the most incredible fidget trickster, but make sure they watch you from a safe distance. Spinners are made from tough stuff that could hurt little ones.

4. Know when to stop
Yes, we know. Fidget spinning can be pretty addictive. If you feel yourself getting tired, take a break, put down the spinner and do something else with your hands. It's always best not to spend too much time on one thing!

ULTIMATE SPINNER FUN!

Can you remember a world without fidget spinners? Nope, us neither! And why would we want to? Spinners are great!

When spinners were first made, they weren't meant to become a worldwide craze. In fact, they were created to help people who had trouble concentrating or fidgeted a lot. Having something to play with releases nervous energy and helps to focus the mind and keep you calm. Now they have become so popular that lots of people like to play with them.

Did you know you can do loads of awesome tricks with spinners, too? Of course you did! Otherwise why did you pick up this book?

If you haven't already done it, take a quick read of our safety rules on the previous page, then read the next page to discover some amazing spinner-science facts. After that, you can learn 40 of the best fidget spinner tricks around. Enjoy!

SPINNER SCIENCE

Ever wondered what makes your spinner so spinny? Take a look inside . . .

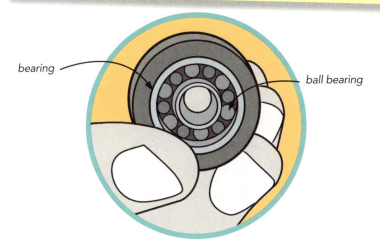

bearing

ball bearing

In the middle of each spinner is a metal wheel, called a bearing, with tiny metal balls inside called ball bearings. This is slotted into the middle of your spinner and covered with a plastic tab.

On the outside of your spinner are three more bearings.

Your spinner moves the way it does because the heavy outer bearings force the ball bearings to spin around.

The speed increases due to the fact that there are three arms on your spinner, creating more weight to push the ball bearings around.

Each part of your spinner needs to be as smooth as possible. Things that are bumpy or rough create friction. The more friction something has, the slower it will be. The ball bearings and wheel-shaped bearings in your spinner are super smooth to make it spin as fast as possible.

Hold your fidget spinner on the tip of your finger with this cool trick!

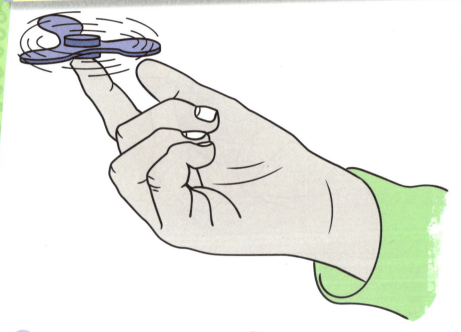

1 Hold your fidget spinner between your thumb and index finger.

2 Get a good spin going!

3 Make sure your index finger is on the bottom of the spinner.

4 Now gently release your thumb until your spinner is balancing on the tip of your index finger!

2 TABLE DROP

This is a great beginner's trick for learning to throw your spinner. Give it a go!

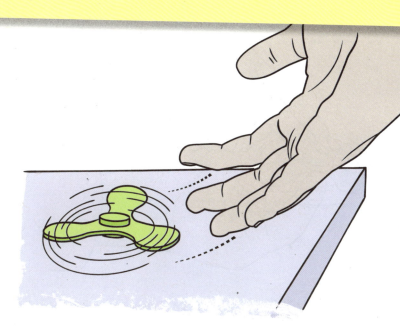

1 Sit by a table or flat surface.

2 Hold your fidget spinner with your index finger and thumb. Make sure your thumb is on top.

3 Start spinning!

4 Toss the spinner onto the table in front of you by releasing both fingers at the same time. Try to keep your spinner level.

5 Your spinner should land on the surface and keep spinning.

TWO-HAND TWISTER

Holding a fidget spinner with one hand is easy, but can you switch from one hand to the other while spinning? Here's how to do it!

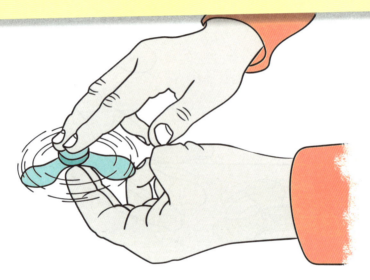

1 Hold the spinner in your right hand with your thumb on the top centre cap and your index and middle fingers on the bottom centre cap.

2 Spin the arms with your left index finger. Then replace your right thumb with your free left index finger so the spinner is held between your left index finger and your right index and middle fingers.

3 Put your left middle finger onto the top centre cap so you're holding the spinner with both your index and middle fingers.

4 Without letting go, turn the spinner over so it is now on top of the fingers of your left hand.

5 Release the fingers of your right hand. Keep practising until you can switch smoothly from one hand to another.

4 CHOPPER SOUNDS

Your fidget spinner doesn't only look cool — it can sound amazing, too! Try this trick to find out how.

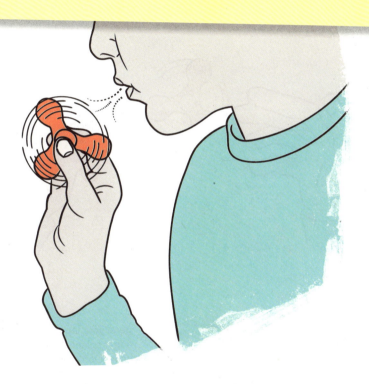

1 Hold the spinner in one hand between your thumb and index finger.

2 Spin it as fast as you can using your other hand.

3 Bring the spinner just in front of your mouth and gently blow onto the rotating blades.

4 Try blowing harder or more gently to see how the sound changes.

HAND TO HAND

This one sounds easy, but it can take a few attempts to get right. Keep going to impress your friends.

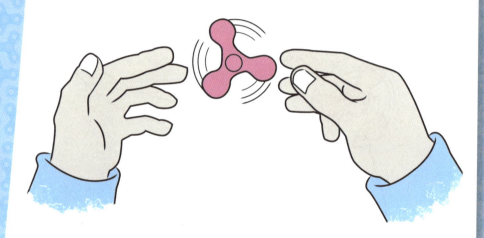

1 Hold your fidget spinner between your thumb and index finger and start spinning.

2 Stand with both arms at waist height with your elbows bent. Get your other hand ready to catch your spinner.

3 Bend your legs and gently toss your fidget spinner over to your other hand. Don't throw it too high.

4 Catch the spinner between the thumb and index finger of your other hand, without stopping it rotating!

6 NOSE PRO

You'll need to take this lying down. Literally!
Find a comfy spot to practise this trick.

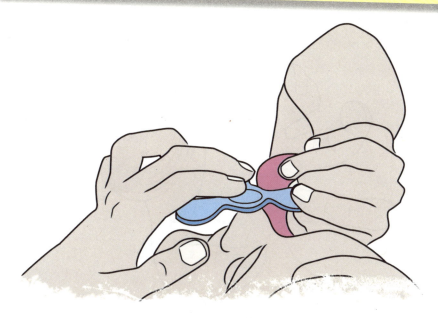

1 Lie on your back so that your nose is pointing in the air.

2 Balance the centre cap of the spinner on the tip of your nose and hold it in place with your index finger.

3 Use your other hand to start spinning.

4 Slowly take your middle finger away so that your nose is the only thing holding your spinner up.

5 Make sure you have found the balancing point before you take your finger away completely.

7 VERTICAL JUMP

Keep your spinner rotating to master this throw-and-catch trick.

1 You can hold your spinner with your thumb and index finger or thumb and middle finger for this trick — whichever feels best.

2 Hold the spinner in a vertical position, like a windmill.

3 Start spinning.

4 Toss the spinner up into the air and catch it again with the same fingers. Your spinner should keep rotating.

BALANCE BOUNCE

Balancing on one finger is easy, right?
Try turning it up a notch . . .

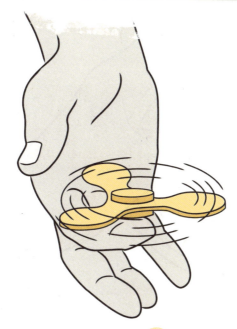

1 Start spinning your spinner.

2 Balance the spinner on the pad of your index finger.

3 Once you feel confident, gently throw the spinner up in the air.

4 Make sure the spinner lands on the same finger.

5 See how many times you can bounce your spinner, then try to beat your score!

STANDING START

If your hands are big enough, try this alternative way to start your spinner rotating.

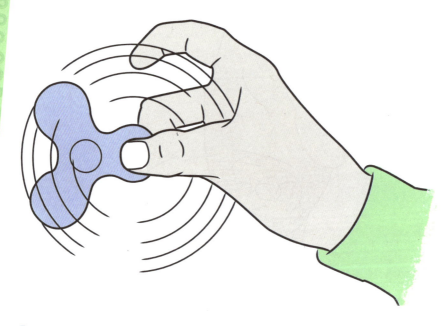

1 Hold your spinner by one of the outer circles using your thumb and middle finger.

2 Toss your spinner vertically into the air to start it rotating. This might take a couple of tries to get right.

3 Catch your spinner in the middle using your thumb and middle finger. Try really hard to keep the rotations going.

ON THE KNUCKLE

It sounds simple, but you'll need perfect hand control for this one.

1 Make your hand into a fist.

2 Balance the middle of your fidget spinner on the knuckle of your index finger, keeping the index finger of your other hand on top.

3 Using your middle finger, start spinning your spinner.

4 Slowly take away your index finger so the spinner is balancing on just your knuckle, and relax your fist.

11 LEAP FROG

Once you've cracked Balance Bounce on page 15, make the jump to the next step!

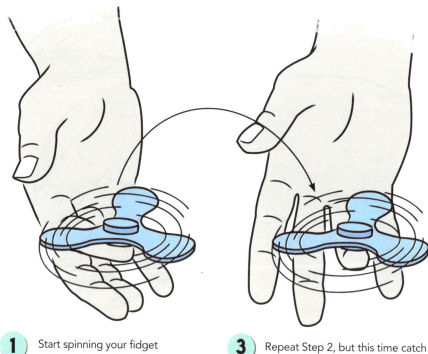

1 Start spinning your fidget spinner on your index finger.

2 While the spinner is at top speed, push it up into the air and catch it on your middle finger.

3 Repeat Step 2, but this time catch the spinner on your third finger.

4 Once you've got the hang of it, try switching the finger order!

12 KNUCKLE FLIP

When you've mastered On the Knuckle on page 17, take your skills to the next level.

1 Start spinning your fidget spinner on your knuckle. If you haven't done this before, turn back to Trick 10.

2 Once you feel like your spinner is steady, thrust it into the air.

3 Flip your hand over and try to catch your spinner on one finger.

4 Once you have mastered this, try going from finger to knuckle, then back again.

13 DOWN UNDER

This can be one of the hardest tricks to master, but one of the coolest to show off!

1 Stand with your legs slightly apart.

2 Start spinning your spinner, holding it between your thumb and index finger.

3 When you feel ready, lift the opposite leg to the hand you are holding your spinner in.

4 Gently toss the spinner under your leg, aiming for your other hand.

5 Catch the spinner with the thumb and index finger of your other hand.

14 PENCIL TOPPER

You'll need an extra-steady hand (and a pencil) for this trick.

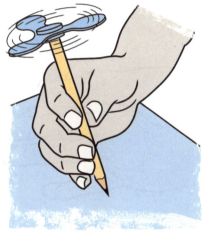

1 Start spinning your fidget spinner between your thumb and index finger.

2 Hold your pencil so the sharp end is facing downwards.

3 Bring your pencil underneath your spinner and gently slide the spinner onto the top of the pencil.

4 Keep your finger on top of the spinner until you feel it will balance.

5 Slowly take away the holding finger.

15 COGS

Get your timing right for this perfect motion trick.

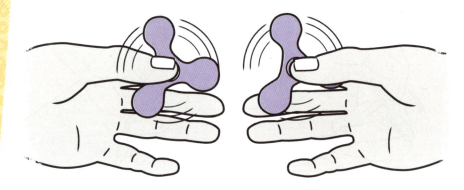

1 Take a fidget spinner in each hand and hold them at a comfortable distance from your body.

2 Kick-start each spinner against your leg or a hard surface.

3 Once spinning, slowly bring your two spinners closer together.

4 Get the timing just right and the outer circles of each spinner will fit together and keep rotating like cogs in a machine.

FLOWER POWER

Create an awesome visual trick with two spinners.

1 Place one fidget spinner on a flat surface (a table would work best) and start spinning.

2 Take another spinner and carefully place it on top of the first spinner. Make sure the bottom spinner doesn't stop rotating.

3 Keeping one finger on top of both spinners, start to spin the top spinner.

4 Look at your spinners from above and you should be able to see a flower shape as the spinners rotate.

17 TOTAL 360

Flexibility and amazing balancing skills are needed for this classic trick.

1 Start spinning your spinner on one finger. It doesn't matter which finger, so choose the one you feel most confident with.

2 When you are ready, slowly turn the palm of your hand towards your body.

3 Move your elbow away from your body to make space for both your hand and fidget spinner to move through.

4 Carry on moving your spinner around until your hand won't go any farther. Then raise and twist your arm while keeping your spinner balanced to complete the full turn.

18 THE TOWER

Get your fidget spinner friends together and see how high you can go!

1 Place your first spinner on a flat surface. A low table is perfect.

2 Start spinning the spinner.

3 Next, take another spinner and place it on top. Keep your finger on the top of the stack.

4 Start spinning the top spinner.

5 Repeat Steps 3 and 4, adding as many spinners as you can.

19 HAND TWIST

Quick hands + precision catching = one amazing trick!

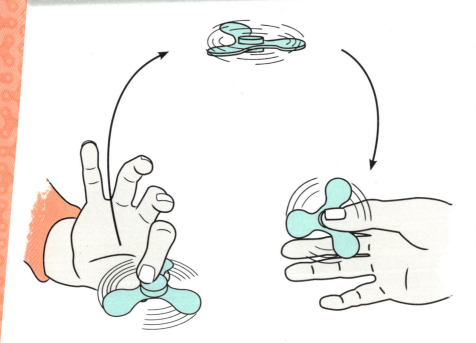

1. Hold your spinner between your thumb and index finger.

2. Start spinning your spinner, then toss it up into the air.

3. While your spinner is airborne, flip the same hand around so that your thumb and index finger have swapped places as you catch your spinner.

TOE GOOD!

Get those feet out for a truly tricky stunt.

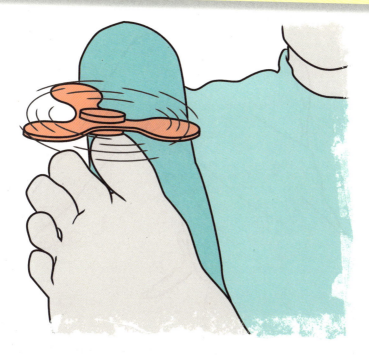

1. Sit on the floor with your shoes and socks off.

2. Rest the heel of your foot on the floor, with your toes pointing upwards.

3. Balance your fidget spinner on your big toe.

4. Once you have the balance right, start spinning. See how long you can keep your spinner in place!

21 HIDE-AND-SEEK

This nifty trick is a must for any serious fidget trickster.

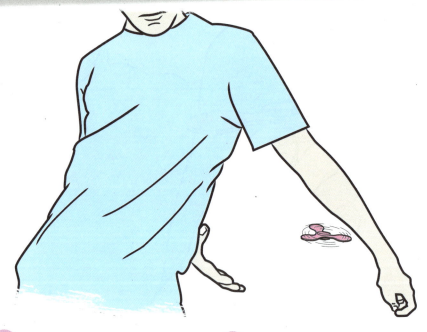

1 While standing, start spinning your spinner in whichever hand feels most comfortable.

2 Push your body forward slightly and toss your spinner behind your back, aiming for your other hand.

3 Try to catch the spinner with your other hand, making sure it is still rotating.

FULL CIRCLE

Sometimes called Around the World, this trick needs super-speedy hands.

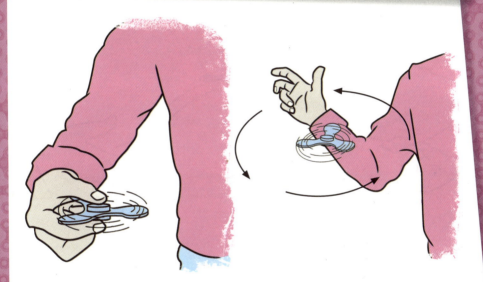

1 Hold your fidget spinner between your thumb and index finger and start spinning.

2 When you are ready, toss the spinner gently in the air.

3 While it is in the air, sweep your hand 360° around your spinner.

4 Catch the spinner with your thumb and index finger again.

23 PLAY CATCH

Find a friend who loves learning tricks as much as you do!

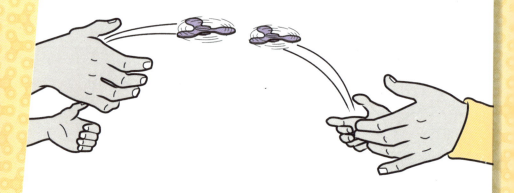

1 Stand facing your friend, a short distance apart.

2 Each of you should start spinning your spinners, holding them however feels most comfortable.

3 Both you and your friend should bend your knees and gently toss your spinners to each other. If you are both right-handed, you should aim diagonally towards your friend's right hand.

4 As the spinners cross in the air you should shift your focus onto your friend's spinner and get ready to catch.

5 Once you have practised a little, try to catch the spinner while it is still spinning.

SWAP-OVER

Your hand-eye coordination will get a great workout with this stunt.

1 Hold a spinner in each hand between your thumb and index finger.

2 Start spinning each spinner.

3 Gently toss each spinner towards your opposite hand. Make sure you throw one over the other to avoid a mid-air crash.

4 Catch each spinner with your opposite hand. When you get really good at this trick, you can try to keep each spinner rotating.

25 OVER ARM

Keep your eyes on the prize and your spinner spinning.

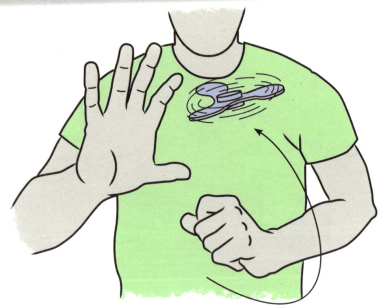

1 Start spinning your spinner in your stronger hand.

2 Hold your free arm out in front of your body.

3 Next, bring your spinning arm under your free arm.

4 Gently toss your spinner up into the air and over your free arm. Then catch the spinner again, making sure it's still spinning!

Turn your spinner into an unidentified flying object.

1 Hold your spinner between your thumb and whichever finger feels most comfortable.

2 Make sure your thumb is on top and start spinning.

3 With the tip of your thumb, make the shape of a circle on the middle of your spinner. Your spinner should begin to wobble and make the shape of a flying saucer.

4 When confident, release your thumb, and your spinner will continue to wobble.

27 CUP CATCH

Find a plastic cup or mug to perform this next stunt.

1 Find an outside space and start spinning your spinner in one hand while holding a cup in the other.

2 Throw the spinner up into the air.

3 Catch the spinner inside your cup.

4 The better you get at this trick, the higher you can throw your spinner. Try catching the spinner in different positions: holding the cup behind your back or under one of your legs.

HOLE-IN-ONE

If your hands are big enough, this is a new way to fidget with your fidget spinner.

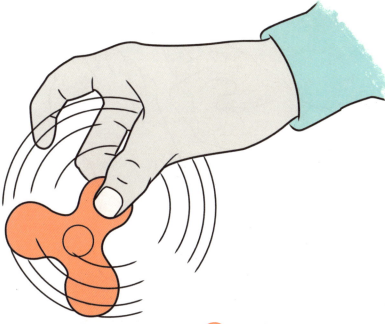

1 Hold your spinner by one of the three outer circles with your thumb and middle finger.

2 Flick your wrist so that the spinner goes up and through the space created by your hand.

3 Keep flicking until your spinner is spinning as fast as you can make it go.

29 TOP-TO-TOE

Once you are a Toe Good pro (master it on page 27), switch it up with this stunt!

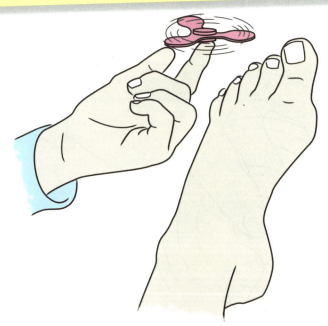

1. Sit on the floor with your shoes and socks off.

2. Start spinning your spinner.

3. Balance your spinner on your strongest finger.

4. Bring your spinner to your foot and position your big toe underneath your spinner.

5. Gently ease your spinner onto your toe and take your hand away.

I'M A FAN!

Feeling hot? Cool down with a fidget-spinner fan!

1 Find a long pole, like a broom handle, bamboo cane or stick from your yard.

2 Start spinning your spinner and gently transfer it onto the end of the stick. (See Trick 14 for more help on how to do this.)

3 Gently raise your stick towards the ceiling.

4 Once it has reached the ceiling, keep it rotating like a ceiling fan!

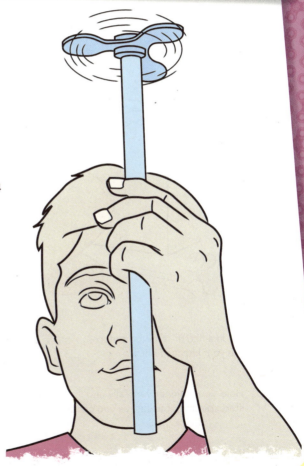

31 WHEELY GOOD

A flick of the wrist and you have motion!

1 Sit on a flat, uncarpeted surface, like your kitchen floor.

2 Hold your spinner vertically and start spinning it as fast as you can.

3 Flick your wrist and release your spinner onto the floor.

4 Your spinner should roll on the floor like a wheel, and it may even come back to you if you have enough spin!

32 BOWLING

Switch up the last trick to play a fun game of bowling.

1 Place some plastic cups on the floor in front of you.

2 Start spinning your spinner while holding it vertically.

3 Release your spinner onto the floor in the direction of your cups. (See Trick 31 for more help on how to do this.)

4 See how many cups you can knock down with a single spinner toss.

Create spiral designs and fidget-spinner originals.

1. Cut out a circle of plain paper about the same size as the circumference of your spinner.

2. Now cut a smaller circle out of the middle of the paper so that it fits over the centre of your spinner.

3. Attach the paper to your spinner using double-sided tape.

4. Start spinning your spinner on a flat surface.

5. Gently touch the spinning paper with a marker, keeping it still as your spinner rotates, to create your design.

6. Add more colours as you go.

34 SPINNER ART 2

The more your spinner moves across the page, the more interesting your design will be.

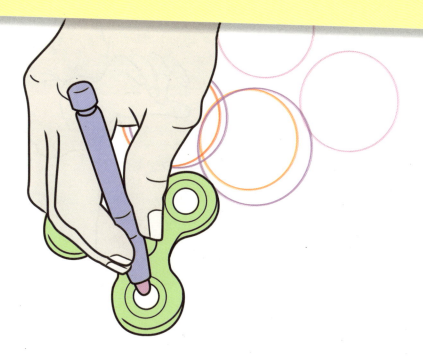

1 Place a sheet of plain paper on a table.

2 Put your fidget spinner on top of the paper and put a pen or pencil through one of the three outer bearings.

3 Use the pen or pencil to start rotating your spinner. This should create a circle on your paper.

4 Wait for the spinner to stop, then choose another colour and start again.

35 LOOP TOSS

Once you've mastered this throw-and-catch trick, it will be your new favourite.

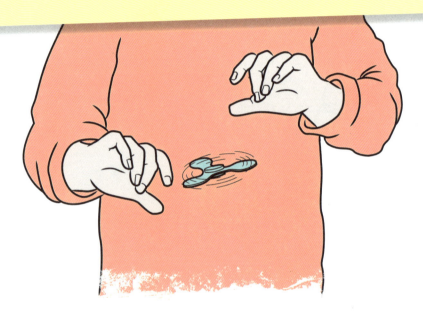

1 Hold your spinner with your thumb and index finger.

2 Start spinning your spinner, then toss it to your other hand. For how to do this, see Trick 5.

3 When you catch your spinner, turn your hand over before tossing it back to the other hand.

4 Continue to toss and turn, creating a smooth looped transition each time.

36 BASKETBALL

Can you rise to the very tip-top for this tricky stunt?

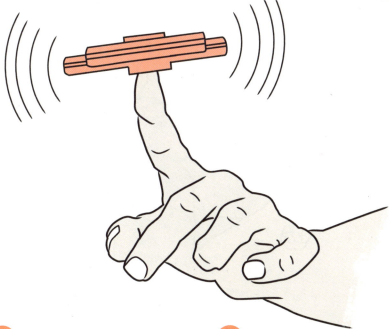

1 Start by spinning your spinner on the pad of your index finger.

2 When you feel confident, start to raise your finger into a more vertical position, while gently bouncing your spinner up and down.

3 Try to bounce your spinner higher, and keep raising your finger until you are able to balance your spinner on the tip.

4 Each time it lands, keep your spinner rotating and try not to let it fall.

If you've got soccer skills, you'll be brilliant at this trick!

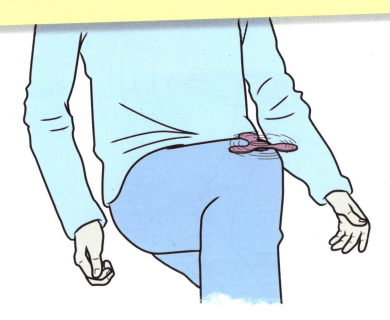

1 While standing up, start spinning your spinner horizontally.

2 When you are ready, drop your spinner onto your knee and try to propel it back into the air (like a game of keep-up).

3 Try to catch your spinner in your hand.

4 Once you can do this with ease, practise keeping your spinner rotating throughout the trick.

38 FLICK BOUNCE

Got the hang of Trick 37? Take it one step further with this slick move.

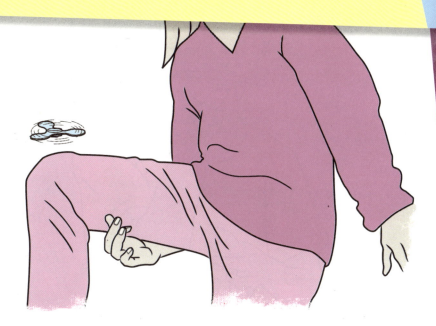

1 While standing, start spinning your spinner in your hand horizontally.

2 Raise your knee, put your hand under your leg and toss your spinner up and over it.

3 As your spinner comes down, knock it back up into the air with your other knee, as in Trick 37.

4 Try to catch your spinner again.

5 As you master the trick, try to keep your spinner rotating throughout.

39 THE DROP

You can make this trick as easy or as hard as you like.

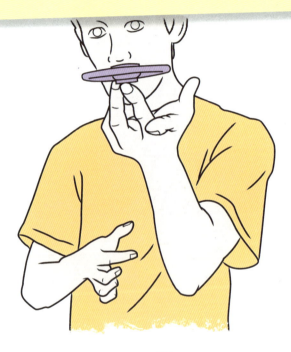

1 Start spinning your spinner on one finger (see Trick 1 for how to do this).

2 Raise your hand as high as you can, then let your spinner drop.

3 Try to catch your spinner with your other hand while keeping it rotating.

4 To make this trick harder, try catching your spinner on one finger, too.

SPINNER SUCCESS CHECKER

Use this page to watch your fidget-spinner skills grow. When your trick starts to gather a crowd, tick it off the list!

1	Finger Hover	○	21	Hide-and-Seek	○
2	Table Drop	○	22	Full Circle	○
3	Two-Hand Twister	○	23	Play Catch	○
4	Chopper Sounds	○	24	Swap-Over	○
5	Hand to Hand	○	25	Over Arm	○
6	Nose Pro	○	26	Spaceship	○
7	Vertical Jump	○	27	Cup Catch	○
8	Balance Bounce	○	28	Hole-in-One	○
9	Standing Start	○	29	Top-to-Toe	○
10	On the Knuckle	○	30	I'm a Fan!	○
11	Leap Frog	○	31	Wheely Good	○
12	Knuckle Flip	○	32	Bowling	○
13	Down Under	○	33	Spinner Art 1	○
14	Pencil Topper	○	34	Spinner Art 2	○
15	Cogs	○	35	Loop Toss	○
16	Flower Power	○	36	Basketball	○
17	Total 360	○	37	Knee Bounce	○
18	The Tower	○	38	Flick Bounce	○
19	Hand Twist	○	39	The Drop	○
20	Toe Good!	○	40	Double Back	○

40 DOUBLE BACK

This stunt can only be achieved by a master trickster. Are you up for the challenge?

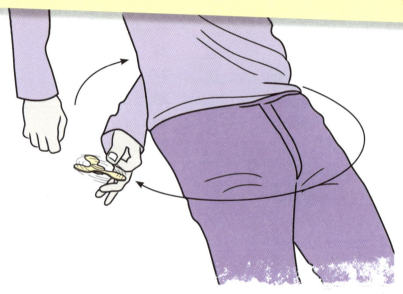

1 In this trick, your spinner moves around your body in a full circle. Start by mastering Trick 21.

2 Now, cross your hands behind your back with the spinner in one hand and the other ready to catch it.

3 Toss your spinner around your side so it curves in front of you.

4 Twist your body so your catching hand behind your back is able to reach your spinner.

5 With practice, you should be able to catch your spinner with your opposite hand snaked around your back.

We Like

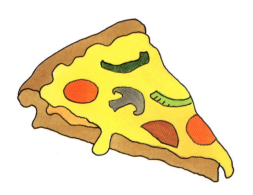

Written by Helen Depree

Illustrated by Bob Kerr

I am Dad.
I like hamburgers.

I am Mom.
I like pizza.

I am Grandma.
I like corn chips.

I am Patch.

I like bones.

I am Sharma.
I like ice cream.

I am Jake.
I like cake.

We all like popcorn.